THE TWELVE STEPS FOR KIDS

Life-changing Steps for Teenagers and Young Adults

by

RON KELLER

illustrated by Gail Steel

Though this book contains no direct quotations from any Bible, I wish to acknowledge that most passages cited are based on texts from the Jerusalem Bible (Doubleday & Company, Garden City, New York), Today's English Version-Good News for Modern Man (American Bible Society, New York, NY), and The New Testament in Modern English, J. B. Phillips (MacMillan Company, New York, NY).

The Twelve Steps for Kids

Copyright © 1989 Prince of Peace Publishing, Inc.

All rights reserved. No portion of this book may be reproduced in any form, except for brief quotations in reviews, without the written permission of the publishers.

Library of Congress Catalog Card Number 89-61180

Keller, J. Ronald, 1945

Bibliography: p.

ISBN 0-933173-20-2

Printed in the United States of America

THE TWELVE STEPS FOR KIDS--A Revolutionary Lifestyle

"It's hard to be a teenager because there are so many pressures put on you to be the 'perfect' person in everyone's eyes..."

Can you benefit from The Twelve Steps for Kids? If you answer "yes" to any of the following questions, you probably can!

- Do you cover up your real feelings?
- Do you feel unloved, afraid? Do you worry?
- Is it difficult to talk with your parents?
- Do you feel lonely? Are you frustrated?

As the traditional Twelve Steps address all of life's major problems and struggles, The Twelve Steps for Kids aim specifically at the issues that tangle and paralyze teenagers and young adults. This book first identifies these problems in all of their peculiar, individual manifestations. It then presents a simple, straightforward approach to the complicated issues facing young people today and creates a forum for discovery, positive change, growth, development, and intimacy with others and with God.

Acknowledgements

I am grateful for Nancy, my understanding wife, and our loving children: Matthew, Brigitte, Peter, Joshua, and Jonathan. For their encouragement and support, I am thankful.

I am grateful for Gail Steel, Mary Wagnild, and all the staff at Prince of Peace Publishing Co. I am also thankful for the support of the staff at the Institute for Christian Living. Their enthusiasm and encouragement have strengthened my own conviction about the importance of this idea.

I respectfully express appreciation to the authors of the original Twelve Steps and to Dr. Vernon J. Bittner for writing <u>The Twelve Steps for Christian Living</u>.

A very special thanks to Brigitte, Peter, Steve, Molly, Dave, Melissa, Amy, Natie, Julie, Steve, Tony, Eileen, Tammy, Carol, Jill, Catherine, John, Daniel, Bob, Matt, Rich, Mark Conway, Bruce Christopher, Rob Hall, Fr. Dennis Evenson, Paul Romstad, and Dorrine Turecamo.

Dedicated to my father, P. J. Keller,
who died on September 22, 1988.
As this work was coming into full life,
his earthly life at age 63 was coming to an end.

What Does the Writer Know About The Twelve Steps for Kids?

Ron Keller has done extensive work with the Twelve-Step process through Ala-Teen, Adult Children of Alcoholics, Al-Anon, small groups, and Twelve Steps for Christian Living groups. As program director for the Institute for Christian Living, he developed and implemented a training program for group leaders.

He was an area/regional director of Young Life for 13 years. He served on the North Dakota State Pardon Board for eleven years, and on the Heartview Alcoholism Treatment Center Board for seven years. Mr. Keller is the former chair of the department of Youth Ministry at Barrington College in Barrington, Rhode Island. He has been a consultant/trainer for Youth Forum, Youth Leadership, Tentmakers, the Catholic Church, Renew, and the Institute for Christian Living. He is an adjunct professor at Luther/Northwestern and Bethel Seminaries in Minneapolis and St. Paul and has an M.A. in Theology from Fuller Seminary. He is also a sailor and a writer. He is the father of three teenagers and two younger boys who are eager to be just like their older brothers and sister.

WHAT'S IN THIS BOOK? (Check the box as you read each chapter)

"It's hard to be a teenager because there are so many pressures put on you to be the "perfect" person in everyone's eyes. You have to have a good head on your shoulders and be happy with yourself. You have to make your own decisions and be careful about the friends you choose..." - Julie

"I am scared and worried. Will there be nuclear war? What is happening to the environment? Will there still be starvation and hardships? What about drug abuse and teenage pregnancy?" - Anonymous

"I am afraid of <u>totally</u> bumming out on life, becoming an addict and making nothing of the life God gave me. I want to live my life to help people and learn about life." - Natie

The Problem

Growing up is tough. Scary. Lonely. Frustrating.

Growing up is complicated and confusing. There are so many decisions to make. And most of them demand choices before kids are ready to make them Most of the important decisions I had to make as a teenager seemed to come before I was equipped to make them.

Growing up is challenging. We have to think carefully about what we should do and who we should spend time with. These mental struggles get even more complicated by the bodily changes that we experience. And all that gets even more difficult when we add the constant invitations to have sex, watch more videos, do drugs and liquor, and listen to more and more heavy music. These and other suggestions come from our peers and within ourselves. "Who should I listen to? How should I act? What should I do and not do? How should I live my life?"

All this can get even more complicated if we don't have a good relationship with our parents, or if our parents are divorced or busy or away from home.

"My biggest problem right now is that I'm too worried about what other people think of me." - Brigitte

How Would You Answer the Questions Below?

Please take a few minutes to answer the questions below. Throughout the book, you'll read answers from other kids. If you need more space, use the blank pages at the back of the book.

My biggest problem right now is:

_____

_____

_____

If I could change one thing in my life right now, it would be:

_____

_____

_____

The biggest mistake I've ever made is:

_____

_____

When I think of my future I feel:

_____

_____

Why?_____

_____

_____

What gets me most excited right now is:

_____

_____

How The Twelve Steps for Kids Can Help You

The original Twelve Steps as well as many other Twelve-Step programs have been used for years and have helped millions of people. The Twelve Steps address all of life's major problems, issues and struggles.

The original Twelve-Step Program was and is still used by alcoholics. The Steps have been a simple, straightforward way for them to get the help they need to stop drinking. The Steps also help them to change those parts of their lives that made their disease worse.

For about thirty years, many other types of people have been benefitting from Twelve Step programs by applying the Steps to their own specific issues and needs.. In groups like Ala-teen, the Steps have helped kids with alcoholic parents to cope with the horrible struggles which often take place in that type of family. Other groups like Narc-Anon, Al-Anon, Overeaters Anonymous, and Emotions Anonymous, to name a few, have also used Twelve-Step programs to improve the lives of their members.

The Twelve Steps for Kids are designed for all kids who need help with daily living. All honest kids know they can use all the help they can get just to make it in life. Besides the issues of daily life, every teenager has an unusual problem or struggle that makes life even more difficult. The Twelve Steps for Kids are helpful to kids any time, but especially when hard times come along.

"What gets me most excited right now is being in sports, going to parties, my family, and just being with friends and girls." - Steve.

How to Use The Twelve Steps for Kids

This book was created for you to use as a tool to help you discover more about yourself. Mark it up!

Read. Read one of the Steps every day. Spend six minutes first thing in the morning and six minutes last thing at night to read or memorize the reading that follows each Step.

Write. Put your thoughts down in the spaces provided. Check off your answers to the questions for each Step. Write or draw in the white spaces. Circle words. Underline phrases. This is your book.

Go Easy. When you go through the Steps, do what you can on each one. Some other time, when you go through the Steps again, you can work on whatever else needs to be done. Don't rush.

Do You Need The Twelve Steps for Kids?

Check those items which are true for you.

_____	Do you feel like you've never had a break in life?
_____	Do you cover up your real feelings? Do you often pretend?
_____	Do you have many unanswered questions about God? Death?
_____	Do you sometimes do or say strange or shocking things just to get attention?
_____	Do you feel unloved, uncared for?
_____	Do you worry about your parents, brothers, and/or sisters?
_____	Do you feel afraid?
_____	Do you avoid going home because you dislike it there?
_____	Do you consider running away from your problems by using drugs, alcohol, or other chemicals or by listening to TV or audio tapes?
_____	Do you go to extremes to get people to like you?
_____	Is it difficult for you to talk with your parents about important things?
_____	Do you feel lonely?
_____	Do you have trouble concentrating on your school work?
_____	Do you lose your temper often?
_____	Do you have some things in your life that you'd like to change and have wanted to change for a long time?
_____	Are there things in your life that you've tried to change but couldn't?
_____	Are you frustrated?

If you checked any of the above statements, you'll benefit from the Twelve Steps for Kids.

© J. Ronald Keller, 1989
Prince of Peace Publishing, Inc.
Burnsville, MN   55337

These Four Things I Know for Sure

1.   We all have problems that we live with every day. Some problems are here today and gone tomorrow, like a bad grade, a fight with a best friend, losing your toothbrush, or missing a party. This kind of problem goes away.

2.   We all have problems that don't go away. They stay with us. *They hurt*. These are problems like death, divorce, fear, loneliness, school problems, personality problems, brother/sister problems, Mom/Dad problems. These problems hang around and never seem to go away. What do we do about them? How do we handle them?

3.   There's a way to live with these "permanent" problems. You can learn a way of life that makes life good even when life's bad.

4.   No matter how hard life is, Jesus Christ has promised that He has come to bring us a full life. You can have that life. The Twelve Steps help kids live a fuller, richer life in all kinds of circumstances.

"When I think of my future, I feel confused because I don't know what's coming next." - Molly

Walking Through The Twelve Steps for Kids is an Adventure

The Steps will call you into honesty like you have never experienced before. *You will discover yourself.* Taking risks and being honest will be very challenging sometimes. Being honest may cause you some pain for a while. But the freedom you find will make the risks and the pain very worthwhile.

This adventure, The Twelve Steps for Kids, is *an adventure with yourself.* You can only work on one person - *you.* The Twelve Steps are *an adventure with God.* You can learn more about His love for you. And the Twelve Steps are *an adventure with others.*

This is a growing process. It's a great idea! It's fun! *And you will be set free!*

How to do The Twelve Steps for Kids

There are three ways to do the Twelve Steps for Kids:

alone,
in a group, or
alone *and* in a group.

Option three is best. It's true that you'll benefit a great deal by doing the Steps alone. However, you'll get the most support and growth by being involved in a group at the same time that you do the Steps yourself.

On page 143, you'll find a group covenant. If there is no group meeting in your area, give this book to an adult friend. Ask that person to help you get a group started. Maybe you're in an existing group that could use these Steps. Suggest that to your group leader.

When you get into the Twelve Steps, use them and apply them to your own life. *You will discover many positive changes* in your attitude toward life: in the way you cope with problems and challenges, in the way that you deal with situations over which you have no control, and in the way that you learn to love those who are "unlovable."

When you get into the Steps, you will learn how to work on changing yourself and developing your own gifts, talents and potential. You will grow.

In your group, you'll find others in the same situation you are in and with similar experiences and feelings. You'll find intimacy with others and with God, and you'll also find fun!

THE TWELVE STEPS FOR KIDS

1. I admit that I am powerless over certain parts of my life and that I need God's help.

2. I am coming to believe that Jesus Christ came in a human body, that He is here with me now in Spirit, and that He has the power to change my weaknesses into strengths.

3. I turn my will and my life over to Jesus Christ, my Savior.

4. I begin honestly listing what I know and discover about myself: my strengths, weaknesses and behavior.

5. I am ready to honestly share with God and another person the exact nature of my strengths, weaknesses, and behavior.

6. I am entirely ready to have Jesus Christ heal all those areas of my life that need his touch.

7. I humbly ask Jesus Christ to change my weaknesses into strengths so that I will become more like Him.

8. I make a list of the people that I have hurt and become willing to go to them to mend the relationship.

9. I make amends with the people that I have hurt, except when to do so might bring harm to them or others.

10. Each day I do a review of myself and my activities. When I am wrong, I quickly admit it. When I am right, I thank God for the guidance.

11. To keep growing in my relationship with Jesus Christ, I spend time each day praying and reading the Bible. I will gather with others who do the same. I ask Jesus for guidance and the power to do what he wants me to do.

12. I am grateful that God is changing me through these Twelve Steps. In response, I will reach out to share Christ's love by practicing these principles in all that I do.

©J. Ronald Keller, 1988
Prince of Peace Publishing, Inc.
Burnsville, MN   55337

"My biggest problem right now is trying to find myself and please others at the same time." - Jill

"My biggest problem right now is lack of confidence in myself. Sometimes I depend too heavily on other people to tell me how I am." - Anonymous

"My biggest problem right now is getting people to like me." - Anonymous

"My biggest problem right now is that I'm in a fight with one of my best friends." - Julie

"My biggest problem right now is establishing myself in a new school." - Matt

"My biggest problem right now is learning how to feel good about the way I am. I'm way too self-conscious." - Anonymous

"My problem is getting my schedule to work out. I'm always very busy and I need to find some time when I can just relax and not worry about all my obligations." - Anonymous

"My biggest problem right now is my family life. It seems that we're always fighting. Every time I turn around they're telling me that I'm a brat or that I'm selfish or they tell me what to do. I'm also having problems with my friends. I seem to get sick of them." - Anonymous

"My biggest problem right now is justifying my existence and trying to find my true purpose in life." - Anonymous

FEELING HOPELESS

STEP ONE

I ADMIT THAT I AM POWERLESS OVER CERTAIN PARTS OF MY LIFE AND THAT I NEED GOD'S HELP.

Feeling Hopeless.......

"You're always feeling bad about your own situation until you run into somebody who's really got it bad. Like, I always felt bad that I couldn't get on the basketball team, until I met this one kid who doesn't even have legs. That's bad." - Tony

It is very important to know ourselves, our problems, and our addictions... what we are powerless over... what we must accept because we cannot change that thing or problem.

It is just as important to *admit* our problems and addictions to ourselves and to God. By denying these parts of ourselves, we deny who we are. When we admit the truth--our powerlessness to change some things--we find freedom, hope, and the strength to cope with things the way they are.

When I was a teenager and living with my family, the biggest problem I had to live with every day was my dad's drinking. He was an alcoholic. I never knew what to expect. Would he be drunk or sober? Did he mean what he was saying or didn't he? Could I count on him or not? Would he embarrass me? His alcoholism affected me in many ways. I was scared about him and his disease. I missed having a father. I was lonely.

When I was fifteen years old, I realized there was nothing I could do about the situation. I couldn't change my dad or anyone else. I could only change myself and the way I looked at things. That first step helped me. It helped me to admit that I was powerless over these circumstances. I had no power to change my dad or myself. I admitted my need for God's help. Fortunately, for the last five years of his life, my dad and I had a great relationship. I discovered many of his good qualities that I hadn't previously recognized. Our relationship had an unusually happy ending.

I am still learning to live with the fact that I will always be powerless over certain parts of my life. Being powerless means I am without power, force, or energy. It means I am weak, that I am not able to produce any effect or change. I am powerless over some of my own personality defects. I'm judgmental. I'm a perfectionist. I'm an ideal-aholic (I think everything should be ideal). I'm a workaholic.

I still admit, *daily*, my need for God's help. I need his help, today more than ever, in little and big things. And I will always need his help.

A page just for you unless you choose to show it to others

<u>My struggles</u>

Check which "addictions" might be yours right now:

_____	TV	_____	Drugs
_____	Phone	_____	Movies/VCR
_____	Feeling guilty	_____	Music
_____	Laziness	_____	Excitement
_____	Sex	_____	Stress
_____	Alcohol	_____	Homework
_____	Chocolate	_____	A relationship
_____	Food	_____	Coca Cola
_____	Sports	_____	Being "cool"

Your main problem today:

_____   My body. I don't like it.
_____   Mom
_____   Dad
_____   What I think about my mom or dad
_____   My brother
_____   My sister
_____   My face
_____   My friend
_____   Boyfriend/girlfriend
_____   Money
_____   School
      _____ Grades
      _____ A teacher
_____   Job
_____   Future
_____   Too many secrets that I need to keep
_____   My past
_____   Others:

_____
_____
_____
_____
_____

Read this passage twice each day and at your meeting.

> I, Jesus, am telling you *not to worry about your life* and what you are to eat, nor about your body and what kind of clothes you are to wear. Surely life means more than food, and the body more than clothing! Look at the birds in the sky. They don't sow or reap or gather into barns; yet the Lord feeds them. Are you not worth much more than they are? Can any of you, for all your worrying, add one single minute to your life span? And why worry about clothing? Think of the flowers growing in the fields; they never have to work or spin; yet I assure you that not even Solomon in all his regalia was robed like one of these. Now if that is how God clothes the grass in the field which is there today and thrown into the furnace tomorrow, will the Lord not much more look after you, you of little faith? So do not worry; do not say, "What are we to eat? What are we to drink? How are we to be clothed?" It is the pagans who set their hearts on all these things. Your heavenly Master knows you need them all. Set your hearts first, on the Lord's kingdom and righteousness, and all these other things will be given you as well. So, don't worry about tomorrow: tomorrow will take care of itself. Each day has enough trouble of its own.

> (Based on Matthew 6: 25-34, JB)

1.   Which situations cause the most worry for you? (Choose one or several.)

_____	Zits	_____	Being grounded
_____	Arguments with Mom/Dad	_____	Having a date
_____	Gossiping friends	_____	Schoolwork/grades
_____	Being alone	_____	My car
_____	My mouth	_____	$$$
_____	_____	_____	_____

2.   Describe a situation in your past where you have felt powerless (you had no power to change the situation).

What did it feel like?

_____

_____

_____

What did you do about it?

_____

_____

3.   In what area of your life do you feel powerless now? How are you handling it?

_____

_____

_____

4.   Have you ever asked for God's help? What happened?

_____

_____

5.   What is Jesus telling you to do in the reading on page 26? What is worth worrying about?

_____

_____

My Reflections on Step One

I admit that I am powerless over certain parts of my live and that I need God's help.

What do you think about Step One? Write down your feelings, thoughts, ideas.

_____

_____

_____

_____

_____

_____

_____

_____

_____

_____

_____

_____

_____

_____

EXERCISE: This week, be brave enough to admit some area of powerlessness. Ask for God's help. Let go. Turn your worries over to him.

For further study:
    Romans 7:15-25
    John 8:34-36
    Romans 8:1-3
    Romans 3:10-14
    I Corinthians 10:12-14

ONE WHO IS GREATER THAN I AM BRINGS HOPE

"If I could change one thing in my life right now it would be my parents' divorce." - Amy

STEP TWO

I AM COMING TO BELIEVE THAT JESUS CHRIST CAME IN A HUMAN BODY, THAT HE IS HERE WITH ME NOW IN SPIRIT, AND THAT HE HAS THE POWER TO CHANGE MY WEAKNESSES INTO STRENGTHS.

Why God? What does God have to do with these Steps?

What is your impression of God right now? (Check those that seem most appropriate for you.)

_____	He's like a parent.
_____	He's like a police officer.
_____	He's the Almighty. He can do everything.
_____	I have my own impression of God that I can't describe.
_____	The best impression I have of God is in Jesus Christ.
_____	He's a distant spirit.

Your God is what you think about most. Who or what is your God right now?

Please look carefully at Step Two. What difference does a Step like this make? *If it's the truth, it'll make all the difference in the world in your life.*

This Second Step is inviting you to relax about where you are at this point in your life. Don't force yourself to be something that you're not or to do something that isn't you. Don't force yourself to believe. Believing is something that comes from within you. It's a gift. It isn't something you force yourself to do. This Step is a reminder that you are who you are. Accept that.

At the same time, you can gradually move toward someone or something. You can "come to believe" by opening yourself up to God, yourself, and others. This Step says that we are *coming* to believe that Jesus Christ came in a body like ours? Is that hard to believe?

The Step says "that He is here with us now in Spirit." If that's true, wouldn't it make all the difference in the world?

This Step also says that Jesus Christ has the power to change our weaknesses into strengths. Whoa!! Is *that* possible? For hundreds of years, people who have called themselves Christians have been saying their weaknesses have been changed into strengths. They say Jesus has done it. Could it be that you too will someday say the same thing?

Joan was born with legs that didn't function. She was disabled from the beginning of her life. She was in hospitals and other institutions most of the time. Her health worsened as time went on. One physical problem led to another. Eventually, one of her legs had to be amputated. The surgery and the aftermath caused many complications.

Joan spent day after day lying in bed and asking, "God, why is it like this? How can I ever be useful to anyone this way?" After a while, it became clear to Joan that she would never get any better. Joan and everyone else around her had to admit that. Her only hope for a better life was to find some way to make her weaknesses her strengths.

Even though Joan was confined to her bed or her wheelchair, she began to use that weakness to her advantage. Two phones, which were donated by several organizations, were installed in her room. One was for business use, the other for personal use. She was able to use those phones and her time to help others.

Everyone has weaknesses. Everyone has strengths. We really don't use our strengths as we could. Our weaknesses often hinder us. Alone, we can do little about them. But God can do great things! He can do the impossible. We get a lot of satisfaction and hope just from being honest enough to admit that we have strengths and weaknesses.

Read this passage twice each day and at your meeting.

As Jesus was getting close to Jericho, there was a blind man sitting at the side of the road begging. He heard the crowd passing by and asked what it was all about. And they told him, "Jesus the Nazarene is going past you."

So the blind man shouted out, "Jesus, Son of David, have pity on me." The people in front scolded him and told him to keep quiet, but he shouted all the louder, "Son of David, have pity on me." So Jesus stood quite still and ordered the man to be brought to him. And when he was quite close, he asked the blind man, *"What do you want me to do for you?"* "Sir," he replied, "let me see again." Jesus said to him, "You can see again! Your faith has saved you." And instantly his sight returned, and he followed him, praising God; and all the people who saw it gave praise to God for what had happened.

(Based on Luke 13:35-43)

Check these out...

1.   Choose one or several. If I had been a blind person at the side of the road, I would have

_____   been quiet and hoped Jesus would have noticed me.
_____   yelled louder and more than the blind man did.
_____   started swinging my fists at everyone who told me to shut up.
_____   kept reading my Braille book, How to Raise Money for the Blind, by I. Have Noeyes.

2.   When Jesus said, "Bring the blind man over here," how would you have felt if you were the blind man?

_____   Relieved.
_____   Snobbish. It'd be about time Jesus would identify the most important people.
_____   Scared.
_____   Humbled.
_____   Embarrassed! Why did I create this scene?
_____   Important! Jesus cares about me!

3.   When have you cried out to Jesus? Did others ever tell you to stop doing that?

_____

_____

_____

4.   If Jesus asked *you* the question, "What do you want me to do for you?" how would you answer it?

_____   I'd ask him to help me in my relationship with my family, especially my _____.
_____   I'd ask him to give me one good friend.
_____   I'd ask him to help me stop this one bad habit.
_____   I'd ask him to take away my pain.
_____   I'd want him to leave me alone.

Think about this...

Here is a man who was born in an obscure village... the child of a peasant woman. He grew up in another obscure village... he worked in a carpenter shop until he was thirty... and then for three years he was an itinerant preacher.

He never wrote a book... he never held an office... he never owned a home... he never had a family... he never went to college... he never put his foot inside a big city... he never traveled more than two hundred miles from the place where he was born... he never did one of the things that usually accompany greatness... he had no credentials but himself... he had nothing to do with this world except the naked power of his divine manhood. While still a young man, the tide of popular opinion turned against him... his friends ran away. One of them denied him... he was turned over to his enemies... he went through the mockery of a trial... he was nailed to a cross between two thieves... his executioners gambled for the only piece of property he had on earth while he was dying... and that was his coat.

When he was dead, he was taken down and laid in a borrowed grave through the pity of a friend.

Nineteen centuries have come and gone and today he is the centerpiece of the human race and the leader of the column of progress.

I am far within the mark when I say that all the armies that ever marched... and all the navies that were built... and all the parliaments that ever sat, and all the kings that ever reigned put together have not affected the life of people upon this earth as powerfully as has that One Solitary Life.

author unknown

And consider this...

Jesus says, I have come to bring you life, life in all its fullness.

Jesus says, I am the way, the truth and the life. No one goes to the Father except by me.

You have been given full life in union with me.

Jesus Christ is the visible expression of the invisible God. He is the first son, superior to all created things. Through Him God created everything in heaven and on earth, the seen and the unseen authorities. God created the whole universe through him and for him. Christ existed before all things, and in union with him all things have their proper place. He is the head of His body, the church. He is the source of the body's life.

God raised Jesus high and gave him the name which is above all other names so that all beings in the heavens, on earth, and in the underworld should bend the knee at the name of Jesus and that every tongue should acclaim Jesus Christ as Lord, to the glory of God the Father.

(Based on John 10:10 and 14:6; Colossians 2:9-10; Colossians 1:15-20; Phillipians 2:9-11)

Rich's story: "There is a reason to live. It took me 16 years to believe this simple idea, that Jesus really is God. That he came in a body like mine. I was raised a Lutheran and I still am one, but it took me all these years to get this idea straight."

A checklist:

1. Jesus Christ came in a body like mine.

    ____ This is hard for me to believe.
    ____ I want to believe it but don't yet.
    ____ This idea is too much for me, but I'm open.
    ____ I believe it.

2. Jesus Christ is with me now in Spirit.

    ____ Never thought about it.
    ____ I've always believed this.
    ____ I want to learn more about this.

3. Jesus Christ has the power to change my weaknesses into strengths.

    ____ I need his help and all the help I can get.
    ____ I don't believe it. I feel like a hopeless cause.
    ____ I want to believe this, but I have no evidence.

"Come near to God, and He will come near to you." (James 4:8)

Your Reflections on Step Two

I am coming to believe that Jesus Christ came in a body like mine, that He is here with me now in Spirit, and that He has the power to change my weaknesses into strengths.

_____

_____

_____

_____

_____

_____

_____

_____

_____

_____

_____

_____

For further study:
  John 3:1-8
  Colossians 1:15-20
  John 1:12-14
  John 3:16
  Romans 8

PUTTING MY TRUST IN SOMEONE GREATER THAN MYSELF

"When I think of my future, I feel scared, questionable." - Brigitte

"I'm trying to be myself when I don't know what myself is." - Eileen

"The thing I am afraid of most right now is not being accepted by peers... or at least having them accept me as I am." - Julie

STEP THREE

I TURN MY WILL AND MY LIFE OVER TO JESUS CHRIST, MY SAVIOR.

When I was in parochial grade school, I was often challenged by the Sisters who taught me. Sometimes I felt encouraged to turn my will and life over to God because of the modeling that they did for me. Most times I didn't feel that way.

As I look back at those experiences, I think that what held me back was fear. I was convinced that if I gave my life to God, I would have to do three things: give up everything I had ever liked, become a priest, and go to Africa.

I have since learned this important truth: that God's will for me will bring me joy. When I am doing His will, I will be enjoying life the most.

I have given my life and will to Jesus Christ. I'm *not* a priest. I have *not* been to Africa (yet), although I've been invited several times, and my life has *not* been miserable because I had to give up everything I have ever liked. In fact, my life has been as rich as it could be. Jesus Christ promises full lives to those who give their lives to God. All those who do turn their lives over to him experience his promises as the truth.

I will admit that I have learned a great deal about giving up things which seem important to me. Maybe your group could talk about their experiences in this area. What has it been like for them to give up things? In comparison, what has Jesus given to you?

"What I am most afraid of right now is facing the high school life of drugs and alcohol." - Steve

Read this twice each day and at your meeting...

One day Jesus got into a boat with his disciples and said to them, "Let's go across to the other side of the lake." They began their journey. As they were sailing, Jesus fell asleep. Suddenly a strong wind blew down on the lake, and the boat began to fill with water. They were all in great danger. The disciples went to Jesus and woke him up saying, "Master, Master, we are about to die." Jesus got up and gave an order to the wind and to the stormy water; they quieted down, and there was a great calm. Then he said to the disciples, "Where is your faith?" But they were amazed and afraid, and said to one another, *"Who is this person? He gives orders to the wind and waves, and they obey him."*

(Based on Luke 8:22-25)

Check these out...

1.   What is your favorite kind of boat?

_____   Powerboat
_____   Sailboat
_____   Fishing boat
_____   Canoe
_____   No boat
_____   A boat sitting safely on shore

2.   What is your favorite body of water?

_____   Lake (name) _____
_____   Ocean _____
_____   River _____
_____   Pond _____

3.   If you had been in this boat with Jesus and the disciples, what might you have done?

_____   Kept sailing, trusting that you'd get to the other side without Jesus' help.
_____   Stayed out of the boat to begin with. I know when storms are coming.
_____   Bailed out when the storm hit.
_____   Called Jesus much earlier.

4.   What is the most difficult "storm" you have ever been "caught" in?

_____

_____

_____

5.   Who helped you in that storm?

_____

_____

6.   In what ways has Jesus saved you?

_____

_____

Step Three, turning our lives over to Jesus, is a hard step. God has given us freedom--freedom to choose. This Step, in one sense, asks us to give that freedom back to God. It asks us to give control of our lives back to him. To surrender. To let go. To let God work in and through us. To let him be Lord.

This Step asks us to trust. Specifically, it asks us to trust Jesus Christ. This Step asks us to give him our wills and our lives. Our wills are our decision-making abilities. Our lives are everything else: our feelings, friends, possessions, problems, ideas, dreams, pain, and this moment. In other words, *everything*.

This is a choice that we make freely and deliberately. It is a choice that we make in stages. The more we get to know Jesus Christ, the more we trust him and give him more of ourselves. This Step may feel a bit scary. There's really nothing to be afraid of. Jesus Christ is the kindest, most gentle, and most loving person history has ever known. He can be trusted.

This is an important Step because there is a lot at stake here. You may decide not to turn your will and life over to Jesus. That means you have decided that you will continue to be your own savior.

God does love you. He does have a plan for you. His plan is rich and full of life. When we turn ourselves over to our Creator, our life is fulfilling. If we hold back, we may be missing out on the great things that God has in store for us.

Ask him to make himself and his plan known to you. Your life will become more directed, and you will become more like him. When you turn your will and life over to Jesus, you will know peace.

Please write your thoughts and feelings about the following:

1.   When I think of turning my will and my life over to Jesus Christ, I feel

_____

_____

_____

_____

_____

_____

2.   List below the names of all the people you know who have been hurt, harmed, or disappointed by Jesus when they have turned their lives over to him.

_____

_____

3.   Indicate where you are with this Step:

_____   I didn't know that Jesus wants my life.
_____   I have given him my will.
_____   I have given him my life.
_____   I don't understand how to do this.
_____   I'm interested but scared.
_____   I don't know where I am with this Step.

4.   Today, what part of you is holding back from turning your will and life over to Jesus Christ?

_____

_____

5.   What does it mean to have Jesus as your Savior? Savior *from* what? Savior *for* what?

_____

_____

_____

_____

My Reflections on Step Three

I turn my will and my life over to Jesus Christ, my Savior.

_____

_____

_____

_____

_____

_____

_____

_____

_____

_____

_____

Exercise:

Turn over as much of your will and your life as you possibly can to Jesus Christ right now. Ask God to help you let go.

For further study:
> Luke 15:11-32
> I Peter 5:7-9
> I John 4:15-17
> I John 5:4-5, 11-13

DISCOVERING ALL OF ME

STEP FOUR

I BEGIN LISTING WHAT I KNOW AND DISCOVER ABOUT MYSELF: MY STRENGTHS, WEAKNESSES, AND BEHAVIOR.

"The worst mistake I've ever made was lying to my Mom." - Amy

"My worst mistake is judging people before I really know them." - Molly

Step Four is about getting to know yourself better. This Step will help you like and love yourself as you are. But you can't love someone or something you don't know. When you know yourself, you will feel more secure, directed, and defined.

Getting to know yourself is a lifelong process. Bit by bit, day by day, you can get a better understanding of who you are. In Step Four, we will clearly and specifically write down what we know and discover about ourselves. Step Four also helps us learn more about our life stories.

When you do Step Four, *begin with now*. Begin with the facts you know are true: that you are loved, gifted, cared for, and created with a purpose, and other things you know about yourself.

Accept yourself as you are. Enjoy who you are.

This Fourth Step is an inventory. That means you count or try to list your strengths and weaknesses. Step Four also asks you to be aware of some of the things you do--your behavior.

Read this twice each day and at your meeting.

You, Oh God, created every part of me. You put me together in my mother's womb. I praise you because you are to be feared. Everything you do is strange and wonderful. I know it with all my heart.

When my bones were being formed and carefully put together in my mother's womb, when I was growing there in secret, you knew that I was there; you saw me before I was born. The days given to me had all been recorded in your book before any of them ever began.

We are God's work of art, created in Jesus Christ.

People don't light a lamp and then hide it or put it under a bowl; instead, they put it on the lampstand so that others may see the light as they come in.

(Based on Psalm 139:13-16; Ephesians 2:10; Luke 11:33-34)

For your response...

1.   When I realize that God created me and is involved with my life right now, I feel

_____   scared.
_____   embarrassed.
_____   excited.
_____   relieved.

2.   When I read what St. Paul wrote about me, that I am "a work of art," I

_____   don't believe it.
_____   don't care. So what else is new?
_____   am grateful for the reminder.
_____   believe it and get excited about it.

3.   When Jesus said "...don't light a lamp and then hide it...", what that means to me is:

_____   I need to use my gifts and talents.
_____   Get fired up.
_____   Get my lamp, light it, and let others see the real me.
_____   I need to get busy finding out where the lamp and the
             light are.

List your strengths and weaknesses. The following pages will help you get started. Add something to the list each day or week.

1.   **Who am I now?**

What do I really like?

_____

_____

_____

_____

What do I really dislike?

_____

_____

_____

_____

What encourages me most?

_____

_____

_____

What discourages me most?

_____

_____

_____

What are my strengths?

_____

_____

_____

_____

_____

_____

_____

_____

What are my weaknesses?

_____

_____

_____

_____

_____

_____

_____

_____

Some things I like about my body...

_____

_____

_____

Some things I like about my mind and the way I think...

_____

_____

_____

Some things I like about my personality...

_____

_____

_____

Some things that I can really do well...

_____

_____

_____

A few things I know I'm not good at...

_____

_____

What I feel I want to do with my life in the future...

_____

_____

Some of the people/things that helped make me the way I am now.

My family (write about your dad, mom, brothers, sisters, and other influential family members):

_____

_____

_____

_____

_____

_____

_____

_____

_____

_____

_____

_____

_____

_____

_____

_____

How I feel about myself (check one, several, or all):

_____	I feel loved as I am.
_____	I feel I'm a good person.
_____	I feel like a bad person.
_____	I feel I need to do things faster than others to be loved.
_____	I feel I need to be perfect to be loved.
_____	I feel I need to be stronger than others to be loved.
_____	I'm OK just as I am. I don't need to change a thing.
_____	All the changes I need to make are very minor.
_____	It's not OK to feel. I have to hide what I feel.
_____	I need to work harder to be loved.
_____	If I want to be loved by others, I need to please them.
_____	It's wrong for me to think about myself and what I want and need out of life.
_____	I'm important.

My feelings about my schools, teachers and classmates
(one-sentence reactions):

Ages 1-5

_____

_____

Ages 6-9

_____

_____

Ages 10-12

_____

_____

Junior High

_____

_____

Senior High

_____

_____

College

_____

_____

Other important stuff about who I am now:

_____

_____

_____

_____

_____

_____

_____

_____

_____

_____

_____

_____

_____

_____

_____

_____

_____

_____

_____

_____

_____

_____

_____

_____

_____

_____

_____

Ask your group leader for more information about available tools to help you get to know yourself better, just as you are right now. Some examples of these tools are Meyers Briggs, DISC, Enneagram, and Hoyt-Wagner Gifts study.

2. **Here's another very important part of doing Step Four: discovering more about who you are now because of Jesus Christ. Look up each of the passages listed below. After reading each one, write down a few words that describe who you are in Christ.**

2 Corinthians 5:17
In Christ, I am _____

Ephesians 4:7 and 1 Corinthians 12:7
In Christ, I am _____

John 3:16
In Christ, I am _____

John 8:32; Romans 8:1
In Christ, I am _____

Revelation 21:1-4
In Christ, I am _____

Colossians 2:9-10
In Christ, I am _____

John 8:1-11
In Christ, I am _____

Ephesians 1:3-14
In Christ, I am _____

_____

_____

_____

_____

_____

_____

_____

_____

_____

_____

3. **My behavior. The last part of Step Four is about what we do or don't do. Answer briefly the questions below.**

    Am I using my gifts?

    _____

    _____

    Am I working on my weaknesses?

    _____

    _____

    What parts of my life are sinful and need forgiveness?

    _____

    _____

    What am I doing that I should not be doing?

    _____

    _____

    What am I *not* doing that I should be doing?

    _____

    _____

    What are my addictions right now?

    _____

    _____

    _____

    _____

My Reflections on Step Four

I begin listing what I know and discover about myself: my strengths, weaknesses, and behavior.

A Fourth Step Prayer

Dear Lord Jesus,
I don't want to kid myself. I want to know who I really am. Even though I am afraid of this some of the time, I really do want to know myself better.

I know I have strengths and weaknesses. That's the way my life is now. I'm sure that's the way it will always be. Help me to be OK with that.

Help me to believe that you love me as I am. Help me to love myself as I am. Help me to love others as they are.

Please give me an understanding of my gifts and talents so that I may properly use them to have a full life and help others in the process.

Thank you, Lord Jesus.

Exercise: Today, begin your lists for Step Four.

For further study:
        Galatians 5
        Romans 12
        Colossians 3:5-17
        John 8:34-36

"The biggest mistake I ever made was lying or not letting my feelings out." - Carol

"The biggest mistake I ever made was to get involved with boys." - Anonymous

"The biggest mistake I ever made was doing drugs because they screwed up my life." - Anonymous

"My biggest mistake was not showing my feelings and telling someone how I felt about them." - Anonymous

"The biggest mistake I've ever made was thinking the popular group has all I ever needed and letting them rule my life. Now I want real friends and they won't let me go." - Jill

"My biggest mistake is continuing to do things with people I know I would regret and not even want to communicate with them later in life." - Catherine

TRUE FRIENDS

Part of Peggy's story:

"I lived a lie most of my life. I ran away from myself and some of the things that I did. I denied so many things about myself and what I did. Finally, I admitted my sin to Jesus. I felt his forgiveness. Then I talked to my best friend. I could trust her. I knew I could.

After talking with her, I got up enough courage to go see my pastor. I told her all about me. Everything. It felt so good to let it all come out... to tell the truth. I am so glad and thankful that I did it."

No one can explain the wonderful freedom that comes to us when we tell the truth to ourselves, to God, and to another person. The relief is beyond description when we discover that we are still loved even though we've done and continue to do some strange things and when we discover that others have the same feelings, fears and ideas.

Admitting to ourselves, God, and another person means there is no more hiding, lying, or denying. Admitting means we have looked squarely into the mirror and that we know who we are, and we accept that.

STEP FIVE

I AM READY TO HONESTLY SHARE WITH GOD AND ANOTHER PERSON THE EXACT NATURE OF MY STRENGTHS, WEAKNESSES, AND BEHAVIOR.

"What I am most afraid of right now is either one of my family will die (including me) or nuclear war." - Dave

All kids have the same desires:

> to have at least one deep, long-term *friend*;
> *to be known* for who they really are by another person, and
> *to know* at least one other person as that person really is.

The Fourth Step reminds us to list what we know about ourselves. The goal is to try to get to know ourselves (our strengths and our weaknesses) better.

Step Five urges us to share what we have discovered with God and with another person. This Step urges us to come clean about who we are. It challenges us to *look* at what we do and maybe *change* some of what we do. It may be that we even need to break away from a habit or from friends who we have discovered are not good for us.

As we talk all this over with God, we will find the forgiveness, peace, and power that we need to live a fuller, healthier, and cleaner life.

Sharing ourselves with a group leader, pastor, counselor, teacher, or trusted friend (older) will help us to find the freedom we need to change our behavior.

Please read this passage twice a day and at your meeting.

> ... get into the habit of admitting your sins to each other and praying for each other...
>
> If we say we have no sin in us, we are kidding ourselves and refusing to admit the truth; but if we freely admit that we have sinned, then God who is faithful and just will forgive our sins and make us thoroughly clean from all that is evil.

(Based on James 5:16; 1 John 1:9-10)

Checklist:

1.   I'm most anxious about sharing myself honestly with

_____   God.
_____   myself.
_____   another person.

2.   In sharing myself with another person, I'm mostly afraid of

_____   being criticized.
_____   being condemned.
_____   being known for who I really am.
_____   being rejected.
_____   being judged.

3.   If I tell someone else who I really am, I believe

_____   they will love me more because they will know more of me.
_____   they will hate me.
_____   they will think less of me.
_____   they will understand.

4.   Have you ever really tried letting someone else know the real you? What was it like?

_____

_____

_____

5.   Think of one person with whom you'd like to share your Fifth Step. Are you willing to make a commitment (to the group) to set up an appointment to go see this person?

_____

_____

_____

Your Reflections on Step Five

I am ready to honestly share with God and another person the exact nature of my strengths, weaknesses and behavior.

St. Paul said, "Jesus Christ came into the world to save sinners, and I myself am the greatest of them" (1 Timothy 1:16).

When Jesus was at dinner in his house, a number of tax collectors and sinners were also sitting at the table with Jesus and his disciples, for there were many of them among his followers. When the scribes of the Pharisees saw him eating with sinners and tax collectors, they said to his disciples, "Why does he eat with tax collectors and sinners?" When Jesus heard this he said to them, "It is not the healthy who need the doctor, but the sick. *I did not come to call the righteous, but sinners.*"

(Based on Mark 2:17)

_____

_____

_____

_____

_____

_____

_____

_____

Exercise: Today, confess your sins to Jesus. Admit them. Let him forgive you and cleanse you completely as he promised.

For further study:
Psalm 32:1-5
John 3:19-21
John 1:29-34
1 John 5:11-13

I WANT MY LIFE TO BE DIFFERENT

"If I could change one thing in my life right now it would be my personality."
- Brigitte

"What I am most afraid of right now is disappointing my parents." - Anonymous

"The biggest mistake I ever made was introducing my friends in 7th grade to my parents. After I did that they wouldn't let me associate with them." - Tony

"Being a teenager is hell because you are treated as a child even though you have overcome this phase in your life..." - Anonymous

"If I could change one thing in my life right now it would be my introvertedness. I want to be more outgoing so I can relate to people better, instead of just sitting back and watching." - Anonymous

"What I am most afraid of is not being true to my feelings." - John

STEP SIX

I AM ENTIRELY READY TO HAVE JESUS CHRIST HEAL ALL THOSE AREAS OF MY LIFE THAT NEED HIS TOUCH.

Everyone hurts. Everyone has areas of their lives that they want changed. Everyone gets fed up with the hurt and those parts of their lives that need to be changed. One day, finally, they get fed up enough to say, "This is it. I give up. I am entirely ready for something different in my life. I've had it. I want to be healed and changed. I don't want to live like this any longer."

Step Six is another Step that reminds us to let go... to surrender... to give up fighting. Jesus comes to us to say, "Let me touch you. Let me heal you."

Being entirely ready brings freedom and liberation. It's important to be ready, *entirely ready*, or little progress and few changes will happen.

"The area in my life that needs to be changed is my temper towards teachers. I get mad too easy." - Dave

Read this twice a day and at your meeting.

> One Sabbath day he was teaching in one of the synagogues, and a woman was there who had been ill for eighteen years. She was bent over double and was quite unable to straighten herself up.
>
> When Jesus noticed her, he called her and said, "You are set free from your illness!" And he put his hands upon her, and at once she stood upright and praised God.
>
> (Based on Luke 13:10-13)

1. Check the statements which are true about this lady:

    _____ She was 18 years old.
    _____ She was bent over double.
    _____ She was a champion tennis player.
    _____ She was unable to straighten up.
    _____ Jesus came to her home.
    _____ Jesus told her she would be set free from her illness.
    _____ Jesus put his hands on her.
    _____ She praised God.

2. Check the statements which are true about you:

    _____ I am a champion tennis player.
    _____ I am bent over double.
    _____ I have a pain/problem that has been with me for a long time.
    _____ I am entirely ready to have Jesus touch me and make my life different.
    _____ I want to be entirely ready, but I don't know how.
    _____ Ready for what? I don't understand.

3. When Jesus says, "You are free from your illness,"

    _____ he meant, "Straighten up, lady, and then I'll help you with your illness."
    _____ he means what he says.
    _____ the lady had to stay doubled over until she said she was sorry for everything she ever did wrong (repent).
    _____ Jesus touched her and healed her because he loved her, and he didn't expect anything in return from her.

4. Look over your lists on Step Four. What part of your life most needs the touch of Jesus?

    _____

    _____

    _____

    _____

    _____

5. What else needs to happen before you'll be entirely ready for Jesus to touch and heal you?

    _____

    _____

    _____

You and Step Six...

We each have to do our part if we want to grow, get healthier, and have a fuller life.

The woman's part was to:

- know what her hurt was,
- get ready to have the hurt healed, and
- get to the place and person who could do the healing

Jesus' part was to:

- respond to our pain.

    He *always* responds; however, he does it in his own time and his own way, not ours. When he saw the woman, he could have ignored her and permitted her to keep her illness. (He did this with Paul, you know, when Paul asked God three times to take the thorn from his side. God did not remove the thorn, but told him that God's grace would be enough to get him through the hard times. In other words, for Paul, it was best for him that his illness--the thorn--be kept in his life. 1 Corinthians 12:7-10). Jesus chose not to do it this way with the woman. Instead, he chose to heal her completely and instantly. He laid his hands on her.

Your part is to:

- get ready. (Identify your areas of need, hurt, and desired changes--Steps Four and Five.)
- get set. Be willing to let Jesus do the healing.
- go! Go to the person who can heal you - Jesus.
- let go. Put yourself and your concerns onto Jesus, and then let him do what is best for you from his viewpoint.

1.   List below the most important changes that you want to take place in your life.

        1)   _____

        2)   _____

        3)   _____

        4)   _____

2.   What is your part in bringing about these changes?

        1)   The change I seek: _____
        What I can do about it: _____
        _____

        2)   The change I seek: _____
        What I can do about it: _____
        _____

        3)   The change I seek: _____
        What I can do about it: _____
        _____

        4)   The change I seek: _____
        What I can do about it: _____
        _____

3.   What are you asking Jesus to do about these areas of your life (his part)?

        1)   _____

        _____

        2)   _____

        _____

        3)   _____

        _____

        4)   _____

        _____

4.   What would you like your group to do to help you make these changes?

_____

_____

_____

_____

_____

_____

_____

_____

_____

_____

My Reflections on Step Six

I am entirely ready to have Jesus Christ heal all those areas of my life that need his touch.

_____

_____

_____

_____

_____

_____

_____

_____

_____

_____

_____

_____

_____

_____

_____

For further study:
    Ephesians 2:3-8
    Matthew 19:26
    Galatians 4:1-11; 5:1
    Acts 3:19-20

"I am probably most afraid of not getting where I want to go because I am afraid of changing my life to do it." - Eileen

"If I could change one thing in my life it would be my feelings of insecurity." - Tammy

"...it's really hard for me to meet the expectations of my family and friends... to be able to do everything my school and friends want me to do." - Anonymous

"Right now I am most afraid of failure." - Daniel

"I am most afraid of failing in front of others, so I never try." - Jill

"I'm afraid most right now to change and try new things. I'm scared I'm going to die, not ever find someone to love, messing up my life with drugs..." - Carol

I ASK FOR MY LIFE TO BE DIFFERENT

STEP SEVEN

I HUMBLY ASK JESUS CHRIST TO CHANGE MY WEAKNESSES INTO STRENGTHS SO THAT I CAN BECOME MORE LIKE HIM.

Lord Jesus,

Through all of these Steps, I come to you with a better understanding of my strengths, weaknesses, shortcomings, and gifts, and also with my sin. I know I have sinned, Lord. Please forgive me. Please do more than forgive me. Please change me so that I can become more like you. I come now to the point where I really need you, probably like I never have before. Please change my weaknesses into strengths.

When I want to criticize, help me to see good things in others.
When I want to lie, please help me to be honest.
When I hate, please help me to love.
When I want to judge others, please have mercy on me, and give me that same mercy for others.
When I want to do wrong, help me to do right.

Lord, please change me. Please take away my bad habits. Replace them with good ones. Please change my heart. Please change my mind. Please change my attitude.

I promise to do my part--to change what I can. But I know that only you have the power to change me and make me like yourself.

I pray that you would do all this, Lord Jesus, in your name.

Read this twice a day and at your meeting.

Jesus said,
Ask, and you will receive; seek, and you will find; knock, and the door will be opened to you.
The one who asks will receive, and anyone who seeks will find, and the door will be opened to the person who knocks.

(Based on Matthew 7:7-9)

1.   Identify one part of your life that you know needs healing. Are you willing to share that with your group?

_____

_____

_____

2.   Have you ever asked Jesus to heal a part of your life before? What was it like?

_____

_____

_____

3.   I want to become more like Jesus.

_____   **Not really.**
_____   Kinda. It would be fun to walk on water.
_____   It's impossible for me. I don't have a chance of ever becoming more like Jesus.
_____   I am going to ask Him to change me so that I can become more like him.

4.   Read the following from Paul:

"With your eyes wide open to the mercies of God, I ask you my dear brothers and sisters to worship God by giving him your bodies as a living sacrifice, consecrated to him and acceptable by him.

Don't let the world around you squeeze you into its own way of doing things, but let God change you into his own mold... by changing your mind from within..."

(Based on Romans 12:1-2)

When I read this passage, I

_____   want to worship God by giving him my body as a living sacrifice.
_____   regret that I have let the world squeeze me into its own way of doing things.
_____   want God to change me by changing my mind from within.

Only Jesus Christ can make these changes. Our role is to ask and to ask *humbly*. He is Lord. He will answer in his own way and in his own time. Asking humbly means we are ready to receive whatever he will give us or withhold from us.

My Reflections on Step Seven

I humbly ask Jesus Christ to change my weaknesses into strengths so that I can become more like him.

Write a letter to God. Ask him humbly to change your weaknesses into strengths.

Dear God:

_____

_____

_____

_____

_____

_____

_____

_____

_____

_____

_____

Your friend,

_____

For further study:
    John 4:43-54
    Psalm 51:1-13
    Matthew 18:1-4

GIVE ME THE GUTS TO GO TO MEND THE RELATIONSHIP

"First I got honest with myself. Then I went to my dad. I had to tell him that I lied. It was so hard, but I had to do it. Everything is OK now again." - Bob

STEP EIGHT

I MAKE A LIST OF THE PEOPLE THAT I HAVE HURT AND BECOME WILLING TO GO TO THEM TO MEND THE RELATIONSHIP.

Make your list of people you have harmed. Begin with those you have hurt today. Gradually work your way back in time so that you include those you have hurt this past week, this month, this year.

Open yourself up to be reminded of someone that you may have hurt quite a while ago. Maybe it was a lie that you told, a rumor that you started. Perhaps you stole something. Maybe you insulted a family member or a teacher.

Look again at your list of behaviors in Step Four. Have you done something wrong to another person? The purpose of Step Eight is to mend the relationship with that person so that you can be free and the relationship can continue.

There is nothing more important than relationships. It is especially important to keep the ones that we have. Our relationships, especially ones with our family, are God's greatest gifts to us. Everything else in life--including material things--mean nothing in comparison to our friendships and relationships. That's why it's so important to be sure that our relationships are "together," mended, united.

We do this because it is the right thing to do. It may not feel good to make this list. It will take courage, but doing this will set you free. We all have a need to be set free, to make amends, to have a clean slate. We all need the peace and relief that comes with knowing that our relationships have been restored.

Take this Step today. Make your list. Get ready to go to mend the relationship.

Please read this several times each day and at your meetings.

Then Jesus came into Jericho and was making his way through it. There he found a wealthy man called Zacchaeus, a chief tax collector, wanting to see what sort of person Jesus was. But the crowd prevented him from doing so, for he was very short. So he ran ahead and climbed up into a sycamore tree to get a view of Jesus as he was heading that way. When Jesus reached the spot, he looked up and saw the man and said, "Zacchaeus, hurry up and come down. I must be your guest today." So Zacchaeus hurriedly climbed down and gladly welcomed him. But those standing by muttered their disapproval saying, "Now Jesus has gone to stay with a real sinner." But Zacchaeus himself stopped and said to the Lord, "Look, sir, I will give half my property to the poor. And if I have cheated anybody out of anything, I will pay him back four times as much." Jesus said to him, "Salvation has come to this house today. *It is the lost that I came to seek and to save.*"

(Based on Luke 19:1-10, Phillips)

1.   Why do you think Zacchaeus was so anxious to see Jesus?

_____   He had everything else in life, and he needed some excitement.
_____   He did a Fourth Step with the Jericho Twelve-Step group and decided it was time to have his life changed.
_____   His life was empty.
_____   He saw the need for Jesus in his life.

2.   Jesus came for the

_____   rich and famous.
_____   short and funny.
_____   lost.
_____   religious people.

3.   Zacchaeus' first vocal response to Jesus was:

_____   I will give half my property to the poor.
_____   If I have cheated anybody out of anything, I will pay him back 10 times.
_____   I never hurt anybody.
_____   I didn't do anything wrong.

4.   Pretend you are Zacchaeus. You have met Jesus, and he has invited himself to your house for lunch. What was your reaction as he invited himself? How does his invitation make you feel?

Does his presence remind you of the need to make amends (as it did for Zach)?

Do you sense Jesus' love for you?

Do you feel ready to make amends because God has come to visit you and let you know that he accepts you as you are?

My list of those I have hurt and with whom I want to mend a relationship:

Family:

_____

_____

_____

Friends:

_____

_____

_____

Relatives:

_____

_____

_____

Teachers:

_____

_____

_____

Pastors:

_____

_____

Others:

_____

_____

_____

"My biggest mistake is not letting myself be all that I could be. I always hold my feelings and thoughts inside, not allowing others besides myself to think about my ideas. I haven't taken advantage of all the opportunities I have been given." - Anonymous

My Reflections on Step Eight

I make a list of the people that I have hurt and become willing to go to them to mend the relationship.

_____

_____

_____

_____

_____

_____

_____

_____

_____

_____

_____

For further study:
John 13:34-35
Matthew 5:20-48
Luke 6:27-28
Matthew 6:12-15
1 Peter 4:7-8

FRIENDS AGAIN

"I regret not being totally honest with myself. I'm trying to change that part of my life right now." - Anonymous

"The biggest mistake I ever made was not telling the truth to my parents, friends, and family. I was not being totally honest with the people I loved. It got me into a lot of trouble and deeply affected me..." - Anonymous

"If I could change one thing in my life it would be my relationships." - Anonymous

"I am afraid of failing in life and my parents being ashamed of me." - Anonymous

STEP NINE

I MAKE AMENDS WITH THE PEOPLE I HAVE HURT, EXCEPT WHEN TO DO SO MIGHT BRING HARM TO THEM OR OTHERS.

You gotta do it now. You can't wait any longer.

Recently a high school student was called out of class by the principal. Someone from the family was waiting in the principal's office. As the student entered, he knew that something very serious had happened. He was right. His father had been killed suddenly in a car accident just a few hours before. The son was overwhelmed. He loved his father dearly. Both father and son were very well-known and liked in the school.

In no time the news spread throughout the school. An unusual thing happened during every break between classes for the rest of that day. At each break, kids were lined up at every available telephone. They were calling their dads to let them know they loved them.

Step Nine reminds us of the urgency in going to people to express our love and concern. Don't hesitate. The importance of being reunited with others cannot be overemphasized. The need is indescribable. Nothing can surpass the wonderful feelings of having restored relationships, of being reconciled.

As people involved in the Twelve Steps, our part is to go to those people with whom we need to restore a relationship. We have to express our feelings, our apologies, our sorrow about the broken relationship. Sometimes we need to go to ask forgiveness. We *always* need to forgive them for what they have done (or not done) to us before we go to them.

Don't *expect* anything from them. Their response is their response--you cannot control it. It would be best if they accept your apology. In some cases, they may not. There is nothing you can do about that. They may reject you. That is the risk you will take. However, you will be at peace inside because you did everything you could to improve the relationship.

Step Nine gives us an excuse to go to others. Usually, the strongest and best relationships we have are the ones that have had a reconciliation, ones where the two parties have come back together after a time of disagreement. Use this Ninth Step as your reason to get closer to the people from whom you have been separated.

The story you are about to read is an important story about one man who had the courage to return to his home to make amends. Read this several times each day and at your meetings.

Once there was a man who had two sons. The younger one said to his father, "Father, give me my share of the property that will come to me in my inheritance." So the father divided up his property between the two sons. Before very long, the younger son collected all his belongings and went off to a foreign land, where he squandered his wealth in wild living.

When he had run through all his money, a terrible famine arose in that country, and he began to feel the pinch. Then he went and hired himself out to one of the citizens of that country, who sent him out into the fields to feed the pigs. He got to the point of longing to stuff himself with pig food, but not a person would offer him anything.

Then he came to his senses and cried aloud, "Dozens of my father's hired men have more food than they can eat, and here I am dying of hunger! I will get up and go back to my father and I will say to him, "Father, I have done wrong in the sight of heaven and in your eyes. I don't deserve to be called your son any more. Please take me on as one of your hired men."

So he got up and went to his father. But while he was still some distance off, his father saw him and his heart went out to him, and he ran and fell and kissed him on his neck . But his son said, "Father, I have done wrong in the sight of heaven and in your eyes. I don't deserve to be called your son any more." "Hurry," called out his father to the servants. "Fetch the best clothes and put them on him! Put a ring on his finger and shoes on his feet. Get that calf we've fattened and kill it and we will have a feast and a celebration! For this is my son. I thought he was dead, and he's alive again. I thought I had lost him and he's found!" And they began to get the festivities going.

(Based on Luke 14:12-13, Phillips)

1.   In this story:

_____   I am like the son, returning to ask forgiveness and to
           make amends.
_____   I am like the father, waiting for someone to return to
           me to make amends.
_____   I can't relate to this story.

2.   The main thing I get out of this story right now is:

_____   Don't ask for your inheritance when you are young.
_____   Jesus is like the father.
_____   How the father forgave the son and was waiting for
           him to return.
_____   I want to go "home" to get things straightened out.

3.   The hardest thing about going to make amends for me is:

_____   making up my mind whether I should go.
_____   making the first move to go.
_____   going.

4.   What holds me back from making amends is:

_____   fear of rejection.
_____   fear of punishment.
_____   it's not worth it.
_____   it's no big deal. I really don't need to go.

5.   For just a few moments, pretend you are the son who returns home after wasting
       his inheritance. What are your feelings as you are walking toward your home
       and you see your father stepping out to meet you? Write about this.

_____

_____

6.   Talk with your group about the most important person that you need to make
       amends with. What is your plan for making amends?

_____

_____

_____

My Reflections on Step Nine

I make amends with the people I have hurt, except when to do so might bring harm to them or others.

_____

_____

_____

_____

_____

_____

_____

_____

_____

_____

_____

_____

Exercise: Today I will go to the first person on my list. I will go, call, or write to make amends.

For further study:
      Romans 13:7-8
      Matthew 5:43-48
      Matthew 6:12
      1 Peter 3:9
      2 Corinthians 5:17-19

"There are lots of things out there--influences--and when I try to be your average teen, I get confused. There are just too many things to look at and to listen to and to feel. I don't like how complex it can get." - Natie

MY DAILY CHECKUP

"My biggest problem today is about school. What I should or shouldn't do in class." - Dave

STEP TEN

EACH DAY I DO A REVIEW OF MYSELF AND MY ACTIVITIES. WHEN I AM WRONG, I QUICKLY ADMIT IT. WHEN I AM RIGHT, I THANK GOD FOR THE GUIDANCE.

I went to parochial schools for grade school and high school. I remember vividly those important days. I'll never forget the hard oak desks and beautifully polished hard oak floors. Specifically, I remember the black boards in our classrooms.

In grade school, the blackboards were used frequently. By the end of the day, the boards were mostly white. One of the students would stay after school to clean the boards with wet rags. As the rest of us left school for the day, we couldn't help but notice how whitened the blackboards had become.

When we returned to school in the morning, the boards were clean. We had a fresh board to work with. The clean boards made me feel good and fresh. I felt like I could start a new day with a clean slate.

It is important for us to clean our personal boards every day. Our hearts and minds need a daily cleansing, just like our bodies do. If I want to live a peaceful life with freedom from guilt, I have to learn how to do a daily review. I have to learn how to let go of one day, how to close the door to it, so I can open the door to another new and fresh day.

Taking a daily review or doing a daily inventory is simple. It is simply a matter of spending the last few minutes of the day reflecting on what that day was like. We need to:

recall people and events in their sequence;
ask God to forgive us;
forgive others if they have hurt us;
ask individuals to forgive us;
thank God for the good things that have happened in
    and around and through us on this day; and
close the door to the day--forgive and forget.

As you do your daily checkup, use these words and phrases to help you evaluate yourself, your day, and your relationships.

_____	Love is patient.
_____	Love is kind.
_____	Love is never jealous.
_____	Love is never boastful or conceited.
_____	Love is never rude or selfish.
_____	Love does not take offense and is not resentful.
_____	Love takes no pleasure in other people's sins or misfortunes; rather, love delights in the truth.
_____	Love is always ready to excuse.
_____	Love trusts.
_____	Love hopes.
_____	Love endures whatever comes.
_____	Love does not come to an end.

The fruits of the Spirit are

_____	love,
_____	joy,
_____	peace,
_____	patience,
_____	kindness,
_____	goodness,
_____	trustfulness,
_____	gentleness, and
_____	self-control.

Love your enemies and pray for those who persecute you.

You must love the Lord your God with all your heart, with all your soul, and with all your mind. You must love your neighbor as yourself.

(Based on 1 Corinthians 13:4-8; Galatians 5:22-23; Matthew 5:43 and 22:37-39, JB)

No human is capable of doing all of this. We all need Jesus Christ to come into our lives, to take over our hearts and lives, and to give us hearts that will be able to do all these important things. When we receive Jesus Christ, he gives us the ability to do what he asks of us. He wouldn't ask us to do something that we're not capable of doing. He, living inside of us, gives us the ability to love, pray, and give of ourselves.

As our relationship with Jesus grows, our ability to love also grows. The more we get to know his love for us, the more we can love other people around us, even if they don't love us in return.

My Reflections on Step Ten

Each day, I do a review of myself and my activities. When I am wrong, I quickly admit it. When I am right, I thank God for the guidance.

For the person who is in Christ Jesus, there is no condemning, blaming, guilt, disapproval, sentencing, judgment. For the person who is in Christ Jesus, there is freedom.

(Based on Romans 8:1)

_____

_____

_____

_____

_____

_____

_____

_____

_____

_____

_____

Exercise: Tonight, before you go to sleep, kneel beside or sit on your bed. Take five minutes to think through the day. Ask God to guide you in your thoughts. Be willing to do what he tells you.

For further study
Romans 8:1
Luke 12:1-3
Ephesians 4:25-26
Phillipians 2:1-4

MY MOST IMPORTANT DAILY APPOINTMENT

"When I think about my future, I feel a little scared because there are so many things that could go wrong." - Melissa

STEP ELEVEN

TO KEEP GROWING IN MY RELATIONSHIP WITH JESUS CHRIST, I SPEND TIME EACH DAY PRAYING AND READING THE BIBLE. I WILL GATHER WITH OTHERS WHO DO THE SAME. I ASK JESUS FOR GUIDANCE AND THE POWER TO DO WHAT HE WANTS ME TO DO.

"I feel nervous, anxious about my future. I feel like I wasted too much of my life already." - Eileen

"When I think of my future, I feel a sense of relief. Finally, I will be on my own." - Anonymous

"When I think of my future, I feel excited. I have become aware that God has plans for me, and that all I have to do is keep myself open to suggestions." - Natie

"I am afraid of adulthood the most. I have no idea of what I want to do or become. Getting a real job and becoming responsible is very frightening." - me

"When I think of my future I feel God will always be on my side and watching over me." - Tammy

Read the following several times each day and at your meetings.

> Ask and you will receive; seek, and you will find; knock, and the door will be opened to you. The one who asks will receive, and anyone who seeks will find, and the door will be opened to the person who knocks.

> There is no need to worry. If there is anything you need, pray for it, asking God for it with prayer and thanksgiving, and that peace of God which is so much greater than we can understand will guard your hearts and minds in Christ Jesus.

> Pray constantly.

> Very early, long before daylight, Jesus got up and left the house. He went out to a lonely place, where he prayed.

> The Spirit comes to help us pray, weak as we are. For we don't know how to pray. The Spirit pleads with God for us in groans that words cannot express.

> ...for where two or three meet in my name, I will be there with them.

> (Based on Matthew 7:7-9; Phillipians 4:6-7; 1 Thessalonians 5:17; Luke 4:42; Romans 8:26; Matthew 18:20)

Think about how you spend your time every day. What is the least important thing you do? How would you like to spend your time? Are you wasting time?

The most important time you can have each day is a time to meet with God. Learn to take time for God. Try an experiment. Meet with God for six minutes each morning and each night. It will become the most important 12 minutes of your day. You will experience peace and guidance like you've never had before. (For help with this, read <u>Mastering Life</u>, a 70-day journal and Scriptural guide.)

1. How do you feel about praying?

   _____ I don't know how to do it.
   _____ I haven't really tried it.
   _____ I want to learn more about it.
   _____ I am undecided about prayer.

2. What phrase from the passages most likely describes where you are?

   _____ I ask, and I know I will receive.
   _____ I don't worry about things. I just ask for what I need.
   _____ I pray constantly.
   _____ I gather with two or three others to pray.
   _____ All of the above.
   _____ None of the above.

3. Share with the group how you feel about praying twelve minutes each day (six minutes in the morning and six minutes at night).

   _____

   _____

   _____

4. What is the next step that you could take to make your relationships with Jesus Christ stronger? Would you be willing to share that with the group?

   _____

   _____

   _____

Step Eleven reminds us that there are five important things we must do if we want to keep growing stronger:

1.   Keep an intimate relationship with Jesus Christ.

2.   Spend time each day praying. Make a list of people, events, and things that you will pray for every day or week. Begin this list below.

The people I want to pray for every day:

_____

_____

_____

_____

_____

_____

_____

_____

_____

_____

_____

_____

The events I want to pray about each day:

_____

_____

_____

_____

_____

_____

_____

_____

_____

_____

Other things I want to pray for each day:

_____

_____

_____

_____

_____

_____

_____

_____

_____

_____

_____

_____

3.   To keep growing, you need to read the Bible every day. Try reading it first thing in the morning and last thing at night. Read the passages in this book. Get yourself a modern translation of the Bible.

When you read the Bible, ask yourself the following questions:

What is the point of this section of the Bible?
What insight into my life does this passage give me?
What do I learn about Jesus?
What action is God asking me to take through this reading?

4.   Get together with peers who are also growing into these things.

5.   Ask Jesus for guidance and the power to do what he wants you to do.

My Reflections on Step Eleven

To keep growing in my relationship with Jesus Christ, I spend time each day praying and reading the Bible. I will gather with others who do the same. I ask Jesus for guidance and the power to do what he wants me to do.

_____

_____

_____

_____

_____

_____

_____

_____

_____

_____

_____

_____

Exercise: Today, I will pray at least twice: once in the morning, and once at night. I will ask God to help me pray more.

For further study:
John 17

REACHING OUT

STEP TWELVE

I AM GRATEFUL THAT GOD IS CHANGING ME THROUGH THESE TWELVE STEPS. IN RESPONSE, I WILL REACH OUT TO SHARE CHRIST'S LOVE BY PRACTICING THESE PRINCIPLES IN ALL THAT I DO.

"I wish I had more time to spend helping the underprivileged, being with friends, volunteering to help others. When you're a teenager, you're constantly being stereotyped by adults, organizations, government, and your friends. Everyone tells you what to do and be. I have a hard time just finding who I am now. We're not really confused, at least, not all the time. I have a definite plan for life and my future. Not all teenagers smoke, party and rebel. I know of hundreds who volunteer, help others and are probably more unselfish than many adults. Teenagers just have a bad reputation. Newspapers never discuss the good, always focusing on the bad. I see 10 minutes during a newscast on a boy who murdered his parents but only 2 or less (or none) on the kid who goes every day to help the elderly. Basically, we want to be loved and respected, just like everyone else. Teenagers shouldn't be ignored, we're the next generation of adults and we've got alot to say." - Carol

There is no greater joy in life than reaching out to others and sharing yourself with them.

When something good has happened to you, it's impossible to hold it in. You want to share that good experience with your family and friends.

If you have sincerely looked at the Twelve Steps, the exercises, your adult leaders, your group, yourself, and your problems, *you most likely have a great deal to be thankful for.*

God uses the Twelve Steps to change people's lives. He uses the Steps to wake these people up, sometimes to shake them up, and sometimes to shape them up. People talk about being restored, renewed, reborn, converted, set free, released, and totally changed through the Twelve Steps. They refer to all of this as having had a "spiritual awakening."

If you've been working these Steps, you too have had a spiritual awakening. It can happen suddenly. For most people it happens gradually, like waking up in the morning. The result of the "awakening" is that you have a growing desire to know and love Jesus Christ. You want to spend more time in his Word, and you want to reach out to serve others.

Your love for God, yourself, and others increases. This is simply because you have begun to grasp a little bit of what God's love for you is like. So, you automatically want to share that love with others. This is wonderful! It's called grace. It's a gift. Thank God for this wonderful gift in your life right now. Thank him for what Jesus Christ has done and is doing for you.

God gives you gifts so that you can share with others. Others need you. Your family and friends need you. Other kids need you. Many kids are so desperate that they are taking their own lives. *You can help. You can make the difference. Bring yourself.* Bring your gifts. Bring Jesus to others. Let him touch others through you.

Read this several times each day and at your meetings:

> As he began to take the road again, a man came running up to Jesus, knelt before him and asked him this question: "Good Master, what must I do to inherit eternal life?" Jesus said to him, "You know the commandments: You must not kill; you must not commit adultery; you must not steal; you must not cheat; you must not bear false witness; honor your father and mother. And the young man said to him, "Master, I have carefully kept these commandments from my earliest days. What is still missing in my life?" Jesus looked steadily at him and loved him, and he said, "There is one thing you lack. Go and sell everything you own and give the money to the poor, and you will have treasures in heaven. Then come follow me." But his face fell at these words and he went away sad, for he was a man of great wealth.
>
> (Based on Mark 10:17-22)

1.   Why did this rich young man come to Jesus?

_____   He was looking for another way to make money.
_____   He was empty. He knew something was missing in his life.
_____   He wanted to find a sure way to heaven.

2.   Which of Jesus' responses to the rich young man impressed you the most?

_____   That Jesus looked steadily at him.
_____   That Jesus loved him.
_____   That Jesus told him how to solve his problem: go sell what he had and give the money to the poor.
_____   That Jesus called him to come and follow him.

3.   Even though the rich young man had carefully kept the commandments from early in his life, one thing was still missing for him. What was it?

_____   His heart was not surrendered to God.
_____   He was good and he was religious, but he had not "sold out" to God.
_____   His wealth was an obstacle.
_____   He did not have a relationship with Jesus Christ.

4.   At this point in the Twelve Steps, what is the one thing that is still missing in your life?

_____   Wealth is an obstacle.
_____   I am not willing to sell everything I have and give the money to the poor.
_____   Eternal life is not that big of a deal to me.
_____   I don't have a good relationship with Jesus Christ.
_____   I don't care much about poor people.

My Twelfth Step - Ways that I/we can reach out

Check below those areas that you *personally* will do something about.

_____	Write a note to Mom.
_____	Write a note to Dad.
_____	Offer to share my resources (computer, games, clothes).
_____	Volunteer my time to help where I am needed.
_____	Write letters to lonely relatives or others I know.
_____	Tell my friends about Jesus Christ.
_____	Write notes to my brother(s)/sister(s).
_____	Call someone to let them know I am thinking of them.
_____	Invite a friend to this group.
_____	Write a note to my teachers.
_____	Help a friend with a project.
_____	Write a letter to a missionary.
_____	Give someone some of my clothes.
_____	Give something valuable away.
_____	Give money to my church.
_____	Pray for everyone in this group every day.
_____	Pray for one country in the world every day.
_____	Give my friend a Bible for his/her birthday.
_____	_____
_____	_____
_____	_____
_____	_____
_____	_____
_____	_____

Check below those you think your *group* should do.

_____   Invite others to come to the group.
_____   Begin a second group (break this one up).
_____   A weekly collection. Give the money to _____.
_____   Get each person in the group a Bible.
_____   Support a mission.
             ____   local
             ____   national
             ____   international
_____   Go on a short trip together.
             ____   city (urban)
             ____   mission
_____   Work on a project to help others.
_____   Go visit shut-ins.
_____   Adopt a grandparent.
_____   Befriend a lonely or rejected kid in school.
_____   Visit a hospital.
_____   Pray for our school(s) and teachers.
_____   Pray for all the kids in our classes.

_____   _____

_____   _____

_____   _____

_____   _____

_____   _____

_____   _____

_____   _____

_____   _____

_____   _____

_____   _____

My Reflections on Step Twelve

I am grateful that God is changing me through these Twelve Steps. In response, I will reach out to share Christ's love by practicing these principles in all that I do.

My Twelfth Step prayer

Dear Lord Jesus,
There is so much to do. So many suffering people need me and my group. Give me the courage to reach out, to give myself to others. Help me to be more like you. Come into my heart, mind, body... all of me. Be my Lord. Help me to be your servant so that I will serve your people as you would want.

I love you, Lord Jesus. I want to love your people as well. Please, day by day, show me how. Amen

_____

_____

_____

_____

_____

_____

_____

_____

_____

_____

Exercise: Today, I will reach out to that one person who has been on my mind.

For further study:
> Matthew 5:13-16
> John 3:1-8
> Matthew 25:31-46
> Luke 15:1-10
> 2 Corinthians 5:17-21